Spy Planes

by Jay Schleifer

Capstone Press

MINNEAPOLIS

Printed in the United States of America.

Capstone Press • 2440 Fernbrook Lane • Minneapolis, MN 55447

Editorial Director   John Coughlan
Managing Editor   Tom Streissguth
Production Editor   James Stapleton
Book Design   Timothy Halldin

Library of Congress Cataloging-in-Publication Data

Schleifer, Jay.
  Spy planes / Jay Schleifer
    p. cm. -- (Wings)
  Includes bibliographical references (p. 44) and index.
  Summary: Discusses the history of surveillance from the sky, describing different types of reconnaissance aircraft and their role in the future.
  ISBN 1-56065-302-7
  1. Reconnaissance aircraft--Juvenile literature. 2. Aerial reconnaissance--Juvenile literature. [1. Reconnaissance aircraft. 2. Aircraft, Military.] I. Title. II. Series: Wings (Minneapolis, Minn.)
  UG1242.R4S35   1996
  358.4'5--dc20   95-11246
                                               CIP
                                               AC

Table of Contents

Chapter 1
Cuba, 1962

The Russian general scanned the clear blue skies over Cuba. He was enjoying the island's warm sunshine and gentle breezes. This island in the Caribbean Sea was one of the most peaceful places he'd ever been stationed.

But his mission was far from peaceful. His orders had been to build a secret missile base on Cuba, just 90 miles (145 kilometers) from the United States. A missile launched from the island could now hit U.S. cities in as little as

A U-2 spy plane displays the black color that helps aircraft evade enemy radar systems.

10 minutes. Russia could win a **nuclear** war against America with one surprise punch.

The general knew that the new base would anger the U.S. government. He worked hard to

keep it secret. His men watched the sky day and night. If a plane appeared, they covered the silos that held the missiles. But they

Many spy planes carry cameras and electronic gear, but no weapons for defense. This makes airborne spying missions very dangerous.

weren't worried. There were no planes to be seen.

There was a plane *out* of sight, though. Some 13 miles (21 kilometers) up, higher than the eye could see, an amazing bird was drifting over Cuba. It had wide wings, a short body, and only a single pilot aboard. And it was painted as black as space.

The most important part of the plane was a set of cameras buried in its belly. These cameras could read a car's license plate from an altitude of 10 miles (16 kilometers). As the plane crossed Cuba, the cameras took hundreds of photographs.

At the plane's base, experts clearly saw the missiles in the photos. They told President John Kennedy, who immediately demanded that the Russians remove the weapons. To show that he meant business, Kennedy ordered U.S. warships to sail to Cuba. Russian submarines then moved into the area.

A war could have started at any moment. Finally, the Russians agreed to pull the

The Russian Tu-16 Badger bomber carries deadly missiles as well as spy cameras.

weapons out. "We were eyeball to eyeball," said one U.S. leader. "And the other fellow just blinked."

The plane with the powerful cameras was the U-2, an American plane. The United States and other nations have protected themselves with the U-2 and other spy planes for many years. Their work is fascinating–and much of it is still top secret.

Chapter 2

The History of Spy Planes

The first warplanes weren't fighters or bombers. They were spy planes. Just before World War I (1914-1918), an Italian captain took off in a tiny craft and flew low over a group of enemy forts. With a clumsy, black camera, he shot photographs of the enemy's weak points. His leaders used the photos to plan an attack. The first airborne spying mission was a success.

The U.S. uses some Phantom fighters as reconnaissance aircraft.

Soon spy planes were flying for all the warring nations. By the end of the war, pilots were taking 12,000 pictures a day. Spying from the air also had gained an official name–aerial **reconnaissance**, or **recon** for short.

Between World War I and World War II (1939-1945), there was peace–and spying. One of the most famous agents of that time was Sidney Cotten, who worked for Britain and France. A businessman, Cotten made many sales trips to Germany in his own plane. Once there, he always offered his best customers a ride. He didn't mention that he would be flying right over German army bases. During the flight, the cameras in his plane took hundreds of photographs.

During World War II, Cotten ran all British spy plane missions. Both sides were examining millions of air recon photos and inventing new ways to take them. One method was to shoot through the windows in the sides of a low-flying plane.

These **side-looking** pictures showed the height of buildings and hills. Side and overhead shots were often combined into a single shot. These **panoramics** gave a clear, complete image of the target area. Studying them was almost like being there.

Pilots flew recon missions before each major battle or bombing run. They also flew missions afterward to show the results. The flights led them right over enemy territory and were extremely dangerous. To save weight and increase speed, the spy planes carried no

A Russian Badger, a twinjet bomber plane, spies on U.S. aircraft carriers in the Pacific Ocean.

weapons. Many pilots never returned from these missions.

Spying continued after the war. Russia flew missions over the United States, England, and Canada, and these nations spied right back. Air recon became **photint** (photo intelligence). Spy cameras used new **infrared (IR)** film that picked up the heat from buildings, vehicles, and the human body. These showed up as glowing shapes in the picture. Because heat

The Mig-25 served the Russian military as a fighter and as a spy plane

travels through clouds and darkness, cameras could use infrared film when regular film would not have worked.

The aircraft also were seeking new information called **sigint** (signals intelligence). All modern armies send electronic signals, such as **radar** and radio waves, into the air. The antennae of sigint aircraft catch and record these signals. They tell where the radars are, what units are on the battleground, and even what enemy leaders are saying during their phone calls.

During the 1991 Gulf War, for example, U.S. experts could have heard Iraqi leader Saddam Hussein yelling at his officers. The U.S. and its allies also sent electronic noise, such as radio static, over the air to confuse the enemy. This kind of electronic warfare is known as jamming.

Other new spy terms are **elint** (electronic intelligence) and **comint** (communications intelligence). The world's spies have a language of their own.

Martin RB-57 Canberra

Over the years, most spy planes have been regular fighters and bombers. Instead of weapons, the planes carried cameras and other gear for their new mission. On U.S. planes, an R for "reconnaissance" is added to the plane's regular name. Some U.S. planes used for spying have been the RF-84F Thunderstreak, RF-101 Voodoo, RF-4 Photo Phantom, and the

An early jet fighter, the Thunderstreak, was fast enough for spying missions.

RB-47 jet bomber. But one of the most important planes the Americans used for spy work came from another nation.

That plane was the Canberra, a medium bomber designed by the British with the help of their allies Canada and Australia. A U.S. company, Martin, bought the plans and redesigned the plane as the RB-57.

Though designed as a bomber, the Canberra was an ideal spy plane. It had a range of 2,300 miles (3,701 kilometers), allowing it to go deep into enemy terrritory. Its two engines ran quietly, even at the plane's top speed of 560 miles (901 kilometers) per hour. The plane also had plenty of room for cameras and listening devices.

For several years, these jets flew directly over Russia and other recon targets. They didn't have the swept wings and needle noses of other military jets. As a result, newspapers seldom printed pictures of the B-57. That was just fine with Canberra pilots.

Chapter 3
Russian Spies

No Russian spy plane has ever flown across the U.S. or Canada the way Canberras and other planes flew over Russia. But Russian planes regularly did fly over Alaska and other areas of the world, such as the Middle East.

Most Russian spy planes are giant bombers. These include the Badger and Blinder jets, and the Bear, a big **turboprop**. The Bear is a long-range plane that can fly up to 28 hours without refueling.

The Russians also use fighters, including the Sukhoi and the MiG-25, one of the fastest planes in the world.

The big Russian Bear is a long-range bomber.

Russian MiG-25 Foxbat

During the 1960s, the Russians heard rumors of a new U.S. superbomber that could fly higher and faster than any MiG. To catch this new plane, they came up with the MiG-25, also known as the Foxbat.

As it turned out, America never built the new superbomber, so the new fighter had nothing to fight. But the Foxbat made a perfect spy plane.

Air-to-air missiles protect the MiG-25 Foxbat. The plane was well-armed but had a limited range.

This MiG is 78 feet (24 meters) long and has a takeoff weight of more than 35 tons. But it can reach 2,100 miles (3,379 kilometers) per hour and fly as high as 16 miles (26 kilometers). Each of the plane's engines delivers more than 25,000 pounds of **thrust**.

Foxbats carry the usual cameras, sigint gear, and **ground-mapping radar**. But they can carry it faster and higher than almost any other plane.

Chapter 4

Dragon Ladies and Blackbirds

Using regular aircraft as spy planes had its limits. The Russian Foxbat, for example, had a range of only 860 miles (1,384 kilometers). That wasn't far enough to spy on places half a world away. Countries needed special planes built for long-range air reconnaissance. For the United States, the U-2 served that purpose.

A jet-powered Blackbird can make the trip across the United States in just over one hour.

Lockheed U-2 "Dragon Lady"

In 1955, an important call came in to Lockheed Aircraft's experimental shop in California. The caller asked Lockheed's top designer, Clarence "Kelly" Johnson, to come to a secret meeting at the White House.

The U-2 was built to survey Russian missile sites.

At the meeting, President Dwight Eisenhower explained that the Russian air force had new missiles. These weapons could shoot down U.S. bombers. "We need a plane that flies so high that no one can touch it," said the President. "Can you build it?"

Johnson agreed to try. He designed a giant glider with huge wings. The plane would have just enough engine power to reach the edge of space. The plane would fly quietly over its target and gather information along the way.

The air force reported that the plane's mission would be to study the weather. But the U (for utility)-2 was not flown by the air force. Instead, U-2 pilots worked for the Central Intelligence Agency **(CIA),** the secret U.S. spy agency. These pilots called the plane the "Dragon Lady."

U-2s flew high over Russia, searching for airfields, missile bases, and rocket launch pads. The Russians could see the Lady coming in on radar, but their missiles always fell short. Then, on May 1, 1960, they shot one down.

The CIA pilot, Gary Powers, carried a poison needle to kill himself in case of capture. But he didn't use it, and the Russians jailed him for spying. Later they exchanged him for a Russian spy the Americans had captured. But there were no more U-2 flights over Russia.

Instead, the U.S. sent the Dragon Lady to other trouble spots. A U-2 found the Russian missile bases in Cuba in 1962. Updated U-2s, renamed TR-1s, still fly secret missions today.

Lockheed SR-71 Blackbird

After the U-2 was shot down over Russia, U.S. experts ordered a plane that would fly higher and faster than Russian missiles. In less than three years, Kelly Johnson and his shop created a new and better spy plane: the SR-71 Blackbird.

Driven by twin engines, the SR-71 blazes across the sky at more than 2,100 miles (3,380 kilometers) per hour. The SR-71 can fly as high as 86,000 feet (26,212 meters), close to outer space. To show what it could do, one SR-71 flew across the entire U.S. in 68 minutes. The trip takes six hours on a passenger jet.

Flying a Blackbird is like going on a space mission. There's a two-day countdown before takeoff, and the crew of two wear space suits. The high speed creates temperatures as high as 1,000 degrees along the skin of the plane.

A Blackbird can survey 100,000 square miles each hour. It takes pictures, gathers sigint, and carries out radar mapping. And it's hard to catch. Not one SR-71 has ever been brought down by enemy action.

Chapter 5

The Highest Eyes in the Sky

At one time, spy pilots worked in tiny cockpits while flying over dangerous territory. Now, many of them fly their craft from the ground. They use remote-control systems and a **joystick** to control reconnaissance aircraft.

Featured Aircraft: RPVs

RPV stands for Remote Piloted Vehicle. These tiny aircraft, also called **drones**, are

In the early 1980s, an F-15 Eagle fighter intercepts a Russian Tu-95 Bear. The invention of pilotless spy aircraft has made these contacts less common.

controlled by radio from the ground. A manned aircraft can also control them from many miles away. Like other spy craft, RPVs carry cameras, radar equipment, and listening devices.

Drones fly missions that no human pilot would survive. These include low-level flights right over an enemy base. They send back video and **data** until they are shot down. RPVs that do make it back land by parachute.

The Blackbird served the Central Intelligence Agency (CIA) as a high-altitude spy plane.

There's no need to worry about a pilot, so RPVs can twist and turn in ways that would kill a human operator. They also race at unbelievable speeds. One drone, the D-21, is launched from the back of an SR-71. The D-21 is faster by far than the world's fastest airplane.

Propeller, jet, or rocket engines power the RPVs. Some fly as high as 102,000 feet (31,089 meters). Others cruise just above the

The Blinder was the first Soviet bomber to fly at supersonic speeds. This made it useful for spying missions.

ground. Canada's Canadair CL-89, an eight-foot long rocket, is one of the most popular drones. It is used by the U.S., France, Germany, and other nations. The CL-89 can send pictures back from up to 43 miles (69 kilometers) away.

Spy Satellites

The highest flying spies in the sky are satellites. Launched by rockets, they circle the globe for months or years at a time. They watch the earth from as high as 22,000 miles (35,404 kilometers). The satellite can take pictures or gather sigint each time the target area passes beneath them. It radios the information to ground stations. It can also send data back in a pod that lands by parachute.

A satellite can be steered with small, built-in rockets. If a war breaks out, operators can change its position. As the earth turns, the battlefield will eventually pass beneath the craft.

How well satellites see is top secret. But you can get an idea from the movie *Clear and Present Danger.* As the hero views a TV picture from a satellite 1,000 miles (1,609 kilometers) up, he sees a man on the ground. He can also see the man's bald spot on the top of his head.

At night or when it's cloudy, satellites go right on spying. They do it by switching from regular to infrared cameras.

Chapter 6

Future Spies

Spy planes and satellites have peered down from the skies for more than 80 years. What's the future of these amazing machines?

Of course, the CIA, the Russian **KGB**, and other spy agencies aren't telling. They won't talk about today's spycraft (or yesterday's). But some information has come out:

• Satellites will be important. No nation owns outer space, so it's lawful to spy from a high orbit. In addition, no nation has ever tried

These Blinders can reach reconnaissance targets in North America with a single refueling.

to shoot down or blind the spy satellite of another nation.

• Sigint will become more important. Computers and other electronic devices now can control weapons, and sigint can keep track of them. It's also safer for spies, who can read electronic signals without going into enemy territory.

• RPVs, which are also safer, will be used more. But there will be times when a spy mission requires a human pilot. The U-2 and SR-71 will stay in service, but new craft will also be built. They'll fly even higher and faster and carry **stealth** technology, which makes some modern fighters and bombers almost invisible to radar.

A Mystery Plane

In early 1995, there were reports of a supersecret new spy plane flying over the Nevada desert. This diamond-shaped mystery craft is said to fly at 3,500 miles (5,633 kilometers) per hour—five times the speed of sound and nearly twice as fast as an SR-71. A new kind of engine that leaves fiery pulses in the sky powers the craft, which is code-named Aurora.

Whether there's an Aurora or not, one thing is sure: spying from the air will go on. In the past, spy planes helped fight wars or prepare for them. But now, air recon is mostly used to prevent war. Every nation sleeps more peacefully knowing that its neighbors are not a threat. When nations can sleep peacefully, they wake to a more peaceful tomorrow.

An RF-4B surveys the skies over Europe, where many nations still fear the power of the Russian military.

The radar pod atop AWACS (airborne warning and control system) planes can watch hundreds of miles of airspace for enemy planes and missiles.

Glossary

CIA–the abbreviation for the Central Intelligence Agency, a U.S. government spy agency

comint–stands for communications intelligence, the mission of listening to enemy radio and phone messages

data–information, often taken from or used by a computer

drone–an aircraft that can be piloted from the ground

elint–stands for electronic intelligence. An important part of elint is finding the source of radar signals

EW–abbreviation for electronic warfare, or jamming enemy messages and radar signals

ground-mapping radar–a type of radar used to draw a map of an area. This system shows hills, valleys, rivers, and other landscape features.

IR–abbreviation for infrared. This kind of photograph records heat instead of light coming from the target. Using infrared, pilots can take photos in darkness or through clouds

joystick–a control handle used to fly planes from the ground

KGB–the abbreviation for Russia's spy agency

nuclear–powered by atomic energy, the same power that heats the sun. A single nuclear-powered bomb or missile can destroy an entire city.

panoramics–recon pictures made up of overhead and side shots. Placed together, the shots create a realistic view of an area

photint–stands for photo intelligence, or reconnaissance pictures

radar–a device that sends electronic beams into the air to locate aircraft in flight

recon–short for reconnaissance

reconnaissance–spying missions. When done from the air, it's called aerial reconnaissance.

RPV–abbreviation for remote piloted vehicle (also called drone). This small aircraft is controlled by radio signals from another location.

side-looking–recon pictures taken from the sides of low flying planes. Side-looking photos can show the height of buildings and hills.

sigint–stands for signals intelligence–listening to electronic signals

stealth–technology that allows an aircraft to be almost invisible to radar

thrust–the amount of power in a jet engine, measured in pounds

turboprop–type of jet engine in which the hot exhaust turns a propeller which, in turn, drives the plane.

To Learn More

Baker, Dr. David. *Spy Planes.* Vero Beach, Florida: Rourke Publishing Group, 1989.

Gann, Ernest K. *The Black Watch: The Men Who Fly America's Secret Spy Planes.* New York: Random House, 1989.

Gunston, Bill. *Spy Planes and Electronic Warfare Aircraft.* New York: Prentice Hall Press/Salamander Books, 1983.

Thornborough, Anthony. *Sky Spies.* London: Arms and Armour Press, 1993.

Walker, Bryce. *Fighting Jets.* New York: Time-Life Books, 1983

Some Useful Addresses

National Air and Space Museum
6th Street and Independence Avenue
Washington, DC 20560

United States Air Force Museum
Wright-Patterson Air Force Base, OH 45433
(Located near Dayton, OH)

National Aviation Museum
P.O. Box 9724
Ottawa, Ontario, Canada KIG 543

Index